D1215227

GONE FOREVER

THE GREAT AUK

by Emily Crofford

CRESTWOOD HOUSE

New York

J
598.33
CROFFORD
1989

LIBRARY OF CONGRESS CATALOGING IN PUBLICATION DATA

Crofford, Emily.
The great auk / by Emily Crofford
p. cm. – (Gone forever)
Includes index.
SUMMARY: Describes how the Great Auk lived before its extinction in the mid 1800s and discusses the physical characteristics, habits, and breeding of other members of the auk family and laws to protect these rare birds.
1. Great auk–Juvenile literature. [1. Great auk. 2. Auks.] I. Title. II. Series.
QL696.C42C76   1989   598'.33–dc20   89-31576
ISBN 0-89686-459-6   CIP
                                                                                        AC

Photo Credits

The Bettmann Archive: 4
Photo Researchers, Inc.: (Stephen J. Krasemann) 7, 20; (Jeff L. Lepore) 13, 14, 16, 17, 21; (George Holton) 15; (Robert W. Hernandez) 18, 19; (Tom McHugh) 29; (Leonard Lee Rue III) 33; (Kenneth W. Fink) 39; (Eric & David Hosking) 45
Culver Pictures, Inc.: 9
Academy of Sciences, Philadelphia: (Steven Holt) 11; (A. Morris) 22; (D. Roby/K. Brink) 25, 26; (O. S. Pettingill, Jr.) 27, 40
DRK Photo: (Don & Pat Valenti) 31
Animals Animals: (Stouffer Productions, Ltd.) 34

Cover illustration by Kristi Schaeppi

Consultant: Professor Robert E. Sloan, Paleontologist
University of Minnesota

Macmillan Publishing Company
866 Third Avenue
New York, NY 10022
Collier Macmillan Canada, Inc.

CRESTWOOD HOUSE

Produced by Carnival Enterprises

Printed in the United States of America

First Edition

10 9 8 7 6 5 4 3 2 1

Macmillan 12/6/91 1095 —c. 2

Contents

The Great Auk stood about 30 inches tall and was a relative of today's puffins and Razorbills.

Before it became extinct in the mid 1800s, the Great Auk was found in the cold waters of the Atlantic Ocean along the coasts of North America and northern Europe.

Extinction

Most of the bird *species* we know today evolved 40 million years ago. The Great Auk was among them. This amazing bird made it through all kinds of climate changes. It even survived when ice covered a third of the earth. The Great Auk was a hardy bird. And it loved the sea.

The Great Auk's first real problem with survival began about 100,000 years ago. That's when Neanderthal man discovered that the big bird was good to eat. We know this

5

because the Neanderthals left well-cleaned bones scattered around their campfires.

About 35,000 years ago, humans carved the Great Auk's figure on the walls of caves. The carvings can now be seen in El Pinto Cave in Spain.

The Great Auk was a swimmer, not a flyer. It stood about 30 inches tall. The Great Auk was a wonderful sight. But now the species is gone forever.

Birds of the Past

Some 200 million years ago, the ancestors of birds were small dinosaurs with scales. To avoid *predators* they skittered up trees and out onto branches. As they evolved, their scales became thinner and lighter, probably to make it easier to dodge between limbs and twigs. Gradually, the scales became feathers.

Quarry workers found the first limestone *fossil* of a true feather in 1861 in Bavaria. The fossil was 150 million years old.

Five other fossils of this first bird were later found from the same and nearby quarries. One was so complete it was like a photograph. Scientists gave the small creature the long name *Archaeopteryx* (prounced ar-key-OP-ter-ix). In Greek that means "ancient wing."

Archaeopteryx had a heavy, roundish body about the size of a crow. It had a long tail. It didn't really fly well. It flapped and glided. Even that was a great advantage. If a predator gave chase on the ground, *Archaeopteryx* could

Over thousands of years, birds adapted to their surroundings. To escape predators, some birds learned to fly, while others became excellent swimmers.

take a long, "flying" leap. If it got cornered in a tree, it could glide to the ground or to another tree.

Evolution works in strange ways. Long before the arrival of *Archaeopteryx*, winged creatures could soar high in the sky. But they weren't birds. They were reptiles called *pterodactyls* (pronounced ter-o-DAK-tils). "Dactyl" comes from the Greek word *daktylos*, which means "finger." The pterodactyl's fourth finger supported its wing. A pterodactyl's leathery wings had no feathers to protect it when the weather turned cold. Feathers protected *Archaeopteryx*.

Archaeopteryx had movable fingers at the top of its wings. The fingers had claws. Some birds still have fingers on their wings, but the fingers aren't useful. *Archaeopteryx* also had sharp teeth. Birds have not had teeth for millions of years. But the *embryo* inside an egg still does.

In time, bird bones became lighter and hollow. Now the only signs that birds were once like reptiles are their scaly, lizardlike legs and that they hatch from eggs.

The Great Auk

The Great Auk stood erect and walked slowly, with the swaying motion of the sea.

The male and female Great Auk looked alike. They were always pictured with large white patches in front of their eyes. That's because people usually saw them during the breeding season. After the breeding season, the white patches disappeared. Instead, a wide white band ran above the eyes and a gray line ran from eye to ear.

The Great Auk wore the same dark coat and gleaming white shirt all year. The chin and throat were blackish brown in summer, white in winter.

Ancient Basque sailors called the big northern seabird *arponaz*. Captain Jacques Cartier and his fellow French explorers called it *apponatz*. Both words mean "spearbill." The Norsemen called it *geirfugl*, or "spearbird."

Spanish and Portuguese people named it *pinguinos*, and French sailors referred to it as *pennegouin*. Those words mean "fat one." The Welsh called it *pingwen*.

During the breeding season, the Great Auk developed large white patches in front of its eyes.

9

Questions about whether these northern birds were true penguins arose when sailors traveled to the Southern Hemisphere. Seeing birds that looked like the Northern Hemisphere penguin, they called them penguins, too.

Birds from both Northern and Southern hemispheres were known as penguins until the northern bird's last days. The islands where the Great Auk had *rookeries* were even called the Penguin Islands. Some *naturalists* still say the Great Auk was the first, and true, penguin.

Scientists who classify birds, however, have decided that only the Southern Hemisphere seabirds were the penguins. The big Northern Hemisphere seabird, they say, was a different kind of bird. It was an auk–a giant auk, or Great Auk. They have classified it in the order Charadriiformes and assigned it to the family Alcidae.

An Auk's Life

To understand how the Great Auk lived before it became *extinct*, we must study its cousins. There are 22 living species of the auk family. *Ornithologists,* or bird experts, often refer to auks as *alcids,* a term that comes from their family name. Alcids include birds such as the auklet, murre, murrelet, guillemot, and puffin. The north Pacific Ocean is their home. Eighteen of the alcid species breed in the north Pacific area, mostly in the Bering Sea. Three of the six species that breed in the north Atlantic also live in the north Pacific.

This model of the Great Auk is on display at the Academy of Sciences in Philadelphia, Pennsylvania.

Most auks breed on oceanic cliffs or islands. During *migration* some species travel thousands of miles from home. In the spring they return to the places where they were born to lay their eggs.

The eggshells come in a wide range of pinks, greens, browns, and grays. The markings may be spots, scrawls, smudges, or streaks. The colors and markings are not to *camouflage* (or hide) the eggs. They make it possible for the auk parents to tell which eggs are theirs and which belong to neighbors of a different species.

Some auks are known by one name in Europe and another in North America. For instance, the auk known as Brünnich's Guillemot in Europe is called the Thick-Billed Murre, or Thick-Bill, in America. It has the biggest population of all auks. The auk called Little Auk in Europe is called the Dovekie in North America.

Since auks depend on the sea for their food, they are good swimmers. Like all birds, they have excellent eyesight. If an auk spots a fish to its liking, it can dive with great speed. By the time the fish senses danger, it's too late to escape.

In addition to fish, auks eat sea worms, eels, shellfish, and seaweed. *Plankton* is an important part of an auk's diet. These microscopic life-forms float with the waves. When plankton freezes in ice, the auks peck it out.

A good supply of small fish is vital to auks. Auks like different species of fish at different depths. The auks vary their diets to prevent food shortages.

On land auks walk in a nearly upright position with a shuffling, awkward gait. With a few exceptions, they nest

Razorbills and auks nest, walk, and rest in an upright position. These Razorbills live on Machias Seal Island in Maine.

in an upright position or at a slight angle. At rest, many auks look as if they're sitting on the backs of their knees.

Most auks breed outside the Arctic Circle, but the Dovekie and some Black Guillemots breed there. The Black Guillemot also breeds off the Pacific and Atlantic coasts. Before the winter ice forms, Black Guillemots set sail for warmer areas. On the western Atlantic, they come as far as New England. Unlike Great Auks, they stick close to shore during migration.

Some auks don't go far from home in the winter. They only move away from the ice to open sea. The Whiskered

Auklet, which breeds on Alaska's Aleutian Islands, stays there all winter.

The Common (or Atlantic) Puffin breeds along the coast of eastern Canada and Newfoundland. It has nesting colonies as far South as the Bay of Fundy, between New Brunswick and Nova Scotia.

The Thick-Billed and Common murres, with rookeries in both the Atlantic and the Pacific, nest shoulder to shoulder. In the Atlantic, the Razorbill (sometimes called the Razorbill Murre) nests with its murre cousins. It is particularly close to the Thick-Bill.

The murres of the auk family enjoy dancing. At the beginning of their dance, they pair off in the water and form

The eastern coasts of Canada, Newfoundland, and Maine are the breeding areas for the Common Puffin.

Auks have small torsos, short necks and legs, and small heads and wings. This Parakeet Auklet is from Alaska.

lines or circles. Then they dive together. They dance underwater by swimming in patterns.

Birds of a Feather

The Great Auk, like other auks, had a chubby torso, small head, short neck, short legs, and small wings. Its three-toed feet were webbed. But each species of auk has some feature that makes it different from other auks.

Some species are small, some large. The smallest auklet is about the size of a sparrow. The biggest auks are the Common Murre, the Thick-Bill, and the Razorbill. The

Of all the auks, the Razorbill looks most like the extinct Great Auk.

Razorbill is 16 inches long; the Thick-Bill and the Common Murre are 17 inches long.

Of all the auks, the Razorbill looks the most like the Great Auk. Its heavy bill is grooved. Its coloring is almost the same as the Great Auk's, but it doesn't have white eye

Razorbills are easily spotted because they each have one narrow white band from the front of their eyes to the top of their beaks.

patches in summer. Instead it has a narrow white band from the front of its eyes to the top of its beak. While it cannot match the Great Auk, the Razorbill is the best diver in the family. The Razorbill can be fierce if its young are threatened.

Parakeet Auklets are short and pudgy and have soft gray patches around their necks.

Most alcids are black and white, but they all have their special differences. The Whiskered Auklet has a plume and a long, graceful whisker growing straight back from each side of its bright orange beak. The short, pudgy Parakeet Auk, with its orange beak, has a soft gray "scarf" at its throat.

The look of an auk changes with the seasons. Auks have three outfits. One is for the spring courting and breeding season. Another is for late summer and fall. The third is for winter.

The biggest differences are between the breeding-season wear and the winter outfit. Some auks' appearance changes more than others. The Black Guillemot makes a complete color change. In summer it's a sooty black, except for a white band across the middle of its wings. In winter it is white, except for black bands at the tops and bottoms of its wings. A black tip on its tail and scattered gray feathers complete the winter outfit.

During the courting season, many auks have markings on their throats and heads. Some grow plumes or crests. Puffins grow bill covers.

The best-known puffin is the Common Puffin, but there are two other species. They are the Horned Puffin and the Tufted Puffin of the north Pacific. The Horned Puffin looks as if it has a horn growing on each upper eyelid. The Tufted Puffin has a curling, golden tuft of feathers on each side of

This Common Puffin was photographed on the coast of Norway.

As many as 40 small fish can fit in the bill of a puffin.

its face. The tufts help it recognize members of its own species when it is time to mate.

The puffin has an interesting-looking bill. It is strongly arched and fat rather than long. When courting time comes, the puffin grows an exotic orange-and-yellow bill cover. The puffin's huge bill carries food to its hungry new chicks. The parent can carry as many as 40 small fish at a time! When the parents go back to sea, they shed the bill covers.

Atlantic Puffins have a sense of fun. Waddling in a group down a grassy cliffside, one may suddenly take to the air. It performs a loop trick, then lands back in the same spot. A

The Horned Puffin looks as if it has horns growing out of each eyelid.

few minutes later the same puffin may repeat the same trick – encore!

The Rhinoceros Auklet has a humped back and always looks sad. During the breeding season, it grows a horn on its beak and a double set of white plumes. It sheds the plumes and horn for the winter months.

Alcid Breeding

Most auks lay only one egg at a time. The male and female take turns *incubating* it. The Ancient Murrelet and the Black Guillemot, however, lay two eggs. The Black Guillemot mother conceals the eggs in crevices. If she can't find a crevice, she digs a nest hole in pebbles.

The puffin father spends less time incubating the egg than other auk fathers do, but even he takes a turn now and then. Puffins only warm the egg at night.

Puffins are quiet during breeding, but the other auks are noisy. They can't sing, but they love to talk. They make an *arrr* or *karr* sound. Depending on the pitch, the sound can be a moan or a grunt, a yelp, or, more likely, talk, talk, talk.

The crowded community where the Razorbill and its murre cousins breed is like a madhouse for a while. Until they get settled, they quarrel and shove each other. Once they have each laid claim to a small space, they tolerate each other.

Both the Common Murre and the Thick-Bill mothers lay their single eggs on bare rock, sometimes within inches of a

Fun-loving Atlantic Puffins waddle in groups around their rocky home.

sheer drop. Don't they worry that they might roll off? Not at all. The eggs are shaped like pears. If the wind rises or if the eggs get bumped, they spin around and stay put.

Razorbills seek out crevices or flat spots with overhangs. The Razorbill egg is oval and will spin rather than roll. The Razorbill does not adopt the upright penguin nesting posture. It crouches low over the egg.

The Dovekie hides its nest and egg under a rock to protect it from arctic foxes and the vicious Herring Gull.

While they will nest in crevices, puffins prefer burrows. With their beaks and claws they dig out a four-to-six-foot-long burrow with a downward slope. At its deepest point, where the mother lays the egg, the burrow is about six feet underground. Sometimes puffins are lucky and don't have to do the tedious digging. They find a rabbit burrow and move in.

The puffin shares a Razorbill trait. It crouches over the egg rather than nesting in an upright position.

Auk chicks stay at home from two weeks to eight weeks, depending on the species. Parent auks use different methods to protect and feed their chicks.

The Dovekie baby stays under its rock until it is time to go out into the world. The parents carry tiny shellfish to it in their cheek pouches. The pouches disappear when their youngster is ready to leave the nest. Since the chick has to be able to fly if it is going to find food, the parents stay with it until its flight muscles are strong.

The young Razorbill stays on its breeding ledge until it is nearly full grown but cannot yet fly. The parents coax it

Common Murres do not make a nest to lay their eggs; they lay them on the bare rock.

Black Guillemot parents do not teach their chicks how to fly. When the chicks are hungry, they will venture toward the sea on their own.

down to the sea and teach it to catch shrimp and small fish.

Most other auk parents also give their chicks fishing lessons. The puffins and the Black Guillemots are exceptions.

For six weeks, puffin parents stuff their offspring with fish, sea urchins, and mussels until their chick weighs more than they do. The parents then go back to sea, leaving the chick to work off some of its weight and develop its flight feathers.

When the youngster is hungry enough, it gets down to the sea. It makes the trip at night because there is less danger from predators.

Black Guillemot parents leave their young ones to keep each other company and take care of themselves.

Adult auks stay with their chicks until the chicks' muscles are strong enough for flight.

A nesting cliff is like a high-rise apartment for auks and other birds. Puffins nest on or near the top where the cliff is covered with soil. Down the cliff breeding gulls, cormorants, gannets, Razorbills, and murres nest on ledges at different levels. The Great Auk nested at the bases of cliffs.

At Home in the Sea

Even at their best, auks are slow fliers. It takes a lot of effort for some auks to get airborne. Even beating their wings as fast as they can, auks can barely get up to 30 miles per hour. The loon, which can reach 90 miles per hour if it is in a hurry, would laugh at the auk's flying skills.

Some of the smaller auks, however, do a great deal of flying. Dovekies fly rather than swim into the Arctic Circle to breed. Ordinarily they spend winters along the Canadian coast. But sometimes they darken the sky as they swarm over Europe and North America on their migrations.

Male and female Great Auks were the same length. Their bodies were heavy and they had the same markings. Like the penguin, the Great Auk had a thick layer of fat to keep it warm in cold seas.

Its black bill was four and one-half inches long, and ridges and furrows crossed both *mandibles*. The bill curved downward near the tip.

For all its weight and bulk, the Great Auk's wings were only six inches long. It could not fly at all.

Once scientists believed some bird species were never

Ridges covered the top and bottom parts of the Great Auk's beak. This model is at the Field Museum in Chicago, Illinois.

able to fly. Now they agree that all birds went through a flying stage. Birds that weren't threatened by predators may have stopped flying. Their bodies grew and their unused wings became smaller. Another theory is that some birds kept the *instinctive* urge to go back into the sea. In the sea their wings became more like fins.

The Great Auk was totally adapted to sea life. It only came on land to breed.

Three hundred years ago the Great Auk lived all across the North Atlantic. It had rookeries from Baffin Bay between Greenland and North America down to the Gulf of

St. Lawrence. In Europe its colonies bred from Norway to the British Isles. In earlier days it had rookeries even farther south. Great Auk bones have been found as far south as Florida and Gibraltar.

When it no longer had rookeries in the Atlantic, the Great Auk continued to make winter trips southward. It swam with its head held high. It wintered off the coasts of France, Spain, and Italy. Florida was also a favorite winter vacation spot.

As with today's birds that fly, the Great Auk knew by some inner clock when the time had come to migrate south. It also knew when it was time to return to its rookeries. One theory is that birds learned to migrate when the great glaciers advanced. It is only a theory, just as are other notions about bird migration. How birds know when the time has come to leave, return, and what path to follow remains a mystery.

The Great Auk was a superb navigator and had an uncanny sense of timing. The spearbirds didn't travel in great flocks the way the smaller auks do. But when nesting time came, they all arrived at their birth sites within a few days.

In its last century, the Great Auk had colonies in places like the Funk Islands off the Newfoundland coast. It nested on Grimsey, Eldey, and other Icelandic islands. Bird rocks in the Gulf of St. Lawrence and St. Kilda of the Hebrides were also good breeding sites.

Though it could not fly in the air, the Great Auk did ''fly'' in the water. It could outrace a rowboat – and outmaneuver

30 *Great Auks developed into fast and powerful swimmers, but because they couldn't fly, their wings became smaller than those of birds that fly.*

one easily. It could bank, veer, change course, twist, and turn. It could dive to depths of 300 feet. It could stay underwater for 15 minutes, longer than a seal could. Or it could float on the waves like a cork. The sea was home – a place to work, play, and sleep.

Sometimes auks hitched a ride on drift ice. Since birds are warm-blooded, wouldn't their feet turn numb or melt the ice enough to become stuck to it like glue? In its usually amazing way, nature saw to it that those things didn't happen. All Arctic birds and mammals have a crosscurrent system in their legs. Their blood systems keep their feet just warm enough to prevent frostbite – but not warm enough to melt ice.

The Great Auks only stayed in colonies when breeding. During migration they traveled in pairs or small groups. Large flocks might gather at points where food was plentiful, but these flocks were nothing like the huge breeding colonies.

Auk Breeding

Little is known about the Great Auk's breeding habits. It laid its egg in late May or early June. Even when the Great Auks nested, they stayed as close to the water as possible. Walking was slow and tedious for them. They depended on the sea for all their food. They only felt safe in the sea.

Auks didn't have to nest on ground that was level with the sea. If it swam very fast, a Great Auk could shoot up out of

Parakeet Auklets, like their auk cousins, depend on water for protection and food.

the water and land on a ledge. It could sail over pack ice in the same way.

The mother laid her single egg on one of the islands used as a rookery. Both parents might rake together a little pile of dried *guano* (or bird droppings) for a nest. Or they might

not even go to that trouble. Auks nested so close together they couldn't move without bumping a neighbor.

The pear-shaped egg was five inches long and three inches across at the widest point. Not all of the Great Auk mothers laid their eggs on the same day. This fact was discovered by "eggers" – people who raided Great Auk rookeries for eggs to sell.

Eggers told of first going to the nesting islands to gather the eggs. Eggs that already had embryos growing inside them were called "foul." The eggers threw them away. Great Auk parents left without eggs would moan and wander aimlessly. The next day the eggers would return and collect the freshly laid eggs.

If that had been the only way people plagued the Great Auk, it would have taken a mighty toll. "The penguin lays but one egg," an egger wrote, "and that being gone lays no more."

Parents took turns with the nesting. Experts think the chick hatched in about six weeks. The parents took turns feeding it. Within two or three weeks, the youngster was ready to learn to swim and find food. The family then abandoned the nest. Altogether, the Great Auks were only on land about eight or nine weeks.

Breeding Great Auks also had to cope with storms and white bears. (These bears were not given the name "polar" until 1800.) White bears swam or rode drift ice to islands where the Great Auks nested. When the white bear had eaten its fill of Great Auks, it became restless and left.

Some Great Auks died in storms and as a result of vol-

The Great Auk laid only one egg a year. If that egg was destroyed, the Great Auk would not lay another one.

canic activity. Iceland and the islands around it are all volcanic. During a volcanic eruption, the sea boils. Lava is thrown everywhere. When it hardens, the lava becomes rock.

T. Ross Browne, who wrote about Iceland's history in the early nineteenth century, gave this account of a volcanic eruption:

> The wild havoc wrought in the conflict of elements was appalling. Birds screamed over the fearful wreck of matter. Columns of spray shot up over the blackened fragments of lava, while in every opening the lashed waters seethed and surged as in a huge caldron.

Beginning of the End

From the time they learned to build seaworthy boats, the people of nearby mainlands knew when to find the Great Auk on land. For the Native Americans of Newfoundland, the spearbird meant food during the long winter. The Great Auk was so important to these people that they carved its image in the bone necklaces they wore.

The men pulled their canoes up to the breeding island. They carried sacks for the eggs. Their paddles were their clubs. They advanced toward the nests.

At first the trusting spearbirds were not alarmed. As the men came closer, the birds became nervous and made defiant croaks. The men began to swing the paddles.

The spearbirds' instinct told them to escape to the water. Another instinct said they must not abandon their mates or their eggs. They could bite, but that was of little help against men with long paddles. The Great Auks were not aggressive by nature. They were gentle, trusting creatures.

When a bird becomes frightened, its temperature soars. The heartbeat and breathing rates increase. The Great Auks panted as they stumbled backward. They bumped into other spearbirds and disturbed their eggs. Those Great Auks bit their own brothers and sisters.

When the egg sacks were full and the hunters had killed as many Great Auks as they could drag away, the men returned to their boats.

Their families ate the eggs and some of the fresh meat. They cut some Great Auks into strips for fish bait. They smoked or dried the rest for food through the winter. The oil from the Great Auks' layers of fat provided light and heat.

Those annual raids made scarcely a dent in the spearbird's population, however. Hungry seafaring men from far away soon posed a greater threat.

Explorers and the Great Auk

Pytheas, a Greek astronomer and geographer, was the first explorer to reach the northern Atlantic. He and his crew went to Iceland in 330 B.C. They no doubt learned that the Great Auk was good to eat.

The Norse chieftain Ottar landed on Iceland's shores in A.D. 890. Marco Polo and his men also discovered the spearbird. So did St. Brendan of Ireland, who called Iceland the Island of Fire. Erik the Red and his son Leif explored Iceland, Greenland, and Baffin Island.

In 1534, a chronicler for the French explorer Jacques Cartier wrote about finding the *apponatz* on the Isle of Birds. "In less than half an hour," he wrote, "our two barcques were laden with them as if laden with stones. Of these each of our ships salted four or five casks, not counting the ones we ate fresh."

Many ships went northward during a gold rush of the 1570s. In one year, 600 Dutch, German, and French ships sailed into the Great Auk's territory. Baffin Island's "gold" turned out to be worthless mica. But still the ships came. There was gold of a sort in whales and in walrus tusks.

Food on sailing ships was scarce, however. Whoever financed the trips allowed just enough food for the crew on the outbound trip. For the return trip the men had to find their own provisions. Getting Great Auks didn't require much effort.

Razorbills have a better chance of survival than the Great Auk did because they do not breed at the water's edge. They stay protected during the breeding season.

Some of the sailors didn't even go to the trouble of dragging them to a boat. Since the Great Auk nested close to the water, all the men had to do was to drop anchor near the island. They ran planks from the ship to the nesting area. They then herded hundreds of Great Auks onto the ship. The ship became a slaughtering pen.

But it was people who had no interest in the spearbird as food who finally *endangered* the Great Auk.

From Need to Greed

Around A.D. 900, people discovered that Great Auks' feathers made fine mattresses. As time went on, the spear-birds' feathers were also used for pillows and sofas. By the mid-1500s, the Great Auk rookeries along the European coasts of the eastern Atlantic were all but gone.

The empty breeding sites alarmed companies in England and America. They needed feathers! They hired crews to search out Great Auk rookeries farther to the north.

The breeding islands became places of horror. Terrified Great Auks were herded into pens by the thousands. They were clubbed one by one and dunked into boiling water to

Without protection, the Atlantic Puffin could face the same grim ending as the Great Auk.

loosen the feathers. If they were still alive after being clubbed, the scalding finished the job. Oil from spearbirds that had already been killed supplied fuel for the boiling pots.

Those spearbirds were the lucky ones. In their mad race to beat out competitors, some feather hunters didn't waste time with killing and scalding. They grabbed Great Auks and plucked them while they were still alive. They tore off pieces of skin along with the feathers. Since they had no interest in the spearbirds as food, they tossed them into the cold sea. Each spearbird died a lingering, painful death.

A Rare Seabird

By 1820, so few Great Auks were left that they became a curiosity. A Professor Fleming of Edinburgh, Scotland, wanted one to show off. He put out word that he would pay well for a live Great Auk.

Two men and two boys in a rowboat were among those searching for the prize. They spotted a lone spearbird on a ledge of St. Kilda. The men went ashore and approached the Great Auk from different directions. It tried to make it to the safety of the sea. One of the boys grabbed it and held on until the others could get there.

They shipped the Great Auk to Professor Fleming and received payment.

The professor fed the spearbird. He tied a string to one of its legs and let it exercise in the sea. The Great Auk broke the string and kept swimming.

It could have died in many ways. It might have drowned if the string became entangled in bottom growth. It might have made a meal for a big fish that could not have caught it normally.

By 1830, the Great Auk was mostly a figure in folktales. Some said it had never existed at all. Then someone discovered that it *still existed.*

Off the coast of Devon, England, lies a foggy island called Lundy. Also called the Isle of Puffins, it is an enormous, flat block of granite surrounded by treacherous currents. Murres had rookeries on the island.

In 1835, a Lundy resident spotted two huge birds like none he had ever seen before. He described them as the "King and Queen of the Razorbill Murres standing up bold-like."

That description perfectly fit the Great Auk. There were reports that a spearbird had been killed on this or that island. As word spread, excitement grew. Wouldn't it be something, people thought, to have the skin and egg of this rare bird?

Someone discovered that the tiny remaining Great Auk population was gathering to breed. They were with some smaller auks on Eldey Island near Iceland.

The Last Days

Collectors commissioned hunters to seek out the spearbird and bring back its skin and its egg.

Within a short time naturalists said that only about 50 Great Auks were left. Museums became alarmed. Future generations might never get to see what the wonderful bird looked like. The museums hired crews to find the Great Auk and bring back specimens to stuff. The hunters did well. They killed and brought back 48 Great Auks.

In 1844, on the island of Eldey, people saw the spearbird for the last time. A pair of auks that museum hunters had missed had returned by instinct to Eldey. The mother had laid an egg. Even though they were among a large group of smaller auks, it was easy enough to spot this pair of Great Auks. They were killed for their skins. While killing the pair, one of the men stepped on the last egg.

The birds were not declared extinct for many years. Naturalists continued to hope and search. An American naturalist-writer, Dr. G. Hartwig, was among them. In 1861, he wrote:

> The last pair of Giant-auks were caught seventeen years ago near the Geirfuglaskers, a group of rocks to the south of the Westman Isles.
>
> Since that time it is said to have been seen by some fisherman, but this is extremely doubtful. The question of its existence can only be solved by a visit to the Geirfuglaskers themselves. That undertaking is attended with extreme difficulty and danger. These rocks are completely isolated in the sea, which even in calm weather breaks with violence against them.

Dr. Hartwig wrote about two Englishmen and an Icelander who had been searching for the Great Auk. The men had hoped to reach the Geirfuglaskers in 1858. They had stayed in the port town of Vestmannaeyjar on Heimaey for several weeks. The fishermen, Dr. Hartwig wrote, were not able ''to undertake the trip because the summer was even stormier than usual.''

Decline of Razorbills and Puffins

When the Great Auk was no longer available, islanders depended on the Razorbill and other seabirds for food and income. Like its famous ancestor, the Razorbill and its egg are good to eat. Its feathers also make good mattress and pillow stuffing.

The Razorbill was not as easily caught as the Great Auk, however. It could fly and nested high on a cliff ledge. *Cropping*, or harvesting, its eggs was difficult.

In the egg season islanders climbed the easiest side of the smaller cliffs or rocks. Some of the men put ropes around their waists. The men lowered the hunters and their egg sacks down the cliffs where the nests were.

When their sacks were full, the egg gatherers tugged on the ropes. Their companions pulled them up. It was a dangerous way to get food. Sometimes the ropes broke and the hunters fell.

The hunters later went to the rock islands to get the tender young Razorbills. According to one account, the men had

Razorbills are hunted for their eggs and feathers, just as Great Auks were hunted. Laws have now been set up to protect Razorbills and to ensure that they will not become extinct.

to do "desperate battle" with the older seabirds. These birds would fight to the death to save their young.

Later hunters found easier ways to kill Razorbills. One way was to put baited planks below the water. The seabirds dived for the fish and broke their necks when they struck the planks.

There is hope for the Razorbill, however. Laws now protect it. It has even come back to an abandoned rookery on the coast of Maine.

Like the Great Auk, the Razorbill, and the pretty Black

45

Guillemot, the puffin is valued for its feathers. It also makes good fish bait.

The Atlantic Puffin is considered the most charming member of the alcids. It is also considered the most stupid. The reason for this is simple. Puffins are curious—and fearless.

The annual hunting of puffins, their eggs, and their young took a heavy toll until laws were passed to stop the practice.

Sadly, the puffin population is still declining. Overfishing of certain school fishes has robbed the puffins of food for their chicks. Other auks have starved.

Cattle and pigs let loose on breeding islands have destroyed puffins, as well. The cattle step on the burrows. The pigs root up the chicks and eat them.

Rats, too, have diminished the puffin population. Rats came onto the breeding islands from infested ships. The rats eat the puffin eggs before the chicks hatch.

Oil spills have taken a terrible toll. When a seabird's feathers become coated with oil, it can't swim or fly. It dies of exhaustion and starvation. In addition, modern fishing nets that are invisible underwater trap many auks. The seabirds can't escape, so they drown.

Dumping wastes in the ocean kills seabirds. Some of the fish filled with toxic chemicals survive. But the birds that eat the fish die.

The World Society for the Protection of Animals, Greenpeace, Friends of the Earth, and other wildlife groups were formed to help save endangered species. Some countries pass laws that punish hunters of protected animals.

Even so, there will always be poachers, people who think it's all right to break laws that protect wildlife. The Razorbill is a favorite target. Some say, "What's the big deal about killing a few Razorbills? There are thousands of them."

People said the same thing about the Great Auk.

For More Information

For more information about the Great Auk, write to:

National Audubon Society
950 Third Avenue
New York, NY 10022

American Museum of Natural History
79th Street and Central Park West
New York, NY 10024

Glossary/Index